DODD, MEAD WONDER BOOKS

Wonders of the Woods

and Desert at Night

By Jacquelyn Berrill

ILLUSTRATED BY THE AUTHOR

DODD, MEAD & COMPANY, NEW YORK

To our children and grandchildren,
all nighthawks in their own way

Contents

I

Nighttime for Animals

Have you ever wondered why you rarely see the animals you know so well from story books and pictures, even when you are way off in the country? Only when the sun goes down and darkness settles over the land, blotting out strange, scary objects, do the shy little creatures gather courage to come from their hiding places in search of food. Many larger animals sleep all day, waiting for darkness to cover them so they can catch the smaller, more timid ones and so satisfy their hunger.

As you may have discovered in my companion book, *Wonders of the Fields and Ponds at Night*, you need not go far from home to meet many of these animal friends. Stand quietly on your porch in the dark and listen and watch. Sounds seem to travel farther in the quiet evening atmosphere, perhaps because the noises of daytime are stilled. Furthermore in the damp night air, odors stay close to the ground and small animals are able not only to hear more clearly the sounds that warn them of danger but also to smell the odors that they have learned to fear. In the nighttime, noses and ears become more important than eyes to many wild creatures.

As you wait, you may see a firefly flash a signal light to a waiting mate or you may watch moths flutter about a shrub. Some insects hide all day from the hungry birds and come out at dusk, when most birds stop looking for food. This is also the time for bats to fly from their sleeping places in dark caves, tall trees and attics to catch the soaring insects.

The barn owl gives an eerie hoot from a nearby tree. You may hear a rustle in the leaves on the ground and instantly the great bird swoops silently down to catch a small mouse for supper. Or the garbage pail turns over with a loud clatter and you know a skunk has made its nightly visit to find what it can to eat. If you watch long enough, you may see the fellow dig about in your flower bed, looking for small animals to add to its meal.

After a day of sleep, all animals are hungry and so early evening is a good time for you to be watching for visitors. Your ears will tell you that the frog concert over at the pond is in full swing and somewhere a whip-poor-will is calling.

If you have read my companion book, you will know about the lives of those creatures that may live near your own home or that may visit your garden in the evening. You will already know how the bat catches tiny insects and at the same time avoids telephone wires. You will know how the mole manages to make the long tunnels across your lawn in the night while you sleep. You will know how the cricket produces its music, and you no longer think of night as completely silent, with everything asleep when you turn out your light. You realize

that the air is filled with beating wings, and that even underground many small animals carry on their busy lives, oblivious of day and night. You already understand that the darkness protects to some extent all the little creatures scurrying about in the grass and bushes and treetops. Yes, the animal world really comes to life while you sleep.

In this book, we are going farther from home, to visit the woods and deserts and plains, to watch the night activities of the animals that live in these more secluded places. Many of

the friends you have met in the garden and fields also live in the forests and great open places. They may look a little different, for they may be larger or smaller or have longer ears, tails or feet. You have seen the cottontail nibble at the young cabbage plants and you may be surprised to find that its relative, the snowshoe hare, has enormous back feet, and that the Jack rabbit has oversized ears. Otherwise, all rabbits are much the same creatures.

The small mouse and the beaver do not look much alike but they are both chisel-toothed animals, or rodents. The mouse has managed to make a life for itself all over the face of the earth where man lives—in woods, desert or your attic, while its much larger relative lives a watery life and manages to be lumberjack, engineer and road builder at the same time.

You will easily recognize the marten and fisher as larger relatives of the weasel. They live most of their lives in the treetops, whereas the smaller weasel is built thin enough to travel through tunnels made by the little field mice. They all belong to the same family and are equally feared by the woods creatures.

The wilder animals are not necessarily strange looking, for the fox and the wolf are much like your neighbor's dog and the large cats, such as the mountain lions, are but wild relatives of your pet kitten.

Most desert animals have their homes underground for protection from the hot sun; their woodland relatives build in the tree tops or hollow stumps. The tiny desert owl swoops quietly from its house in a cactus plant and the great horned owl of the forest drops as silently from the entrance hole in a treetop dwelling. Materials available near their home locations are always used for food and construction. For instance, the desert rat makes a fortress of sharp cactus spines and the muskrat builds its castle of cattails. Woodland animals have plenty of leaves and branches for their nests, trees to climb and underbrush to hide in. They have fruit and berries and leaves and roots for food, if they are vegetarians, and for those that are meat eaters there are deep, dark shadows to cover them while

The tiny desert owl takes an insect to its nest in a cactus plant.

11

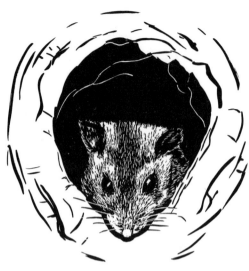

A shy whitefoot mouse looks around carefully before venturing out.

they lie waiting for their prey.

Perhaps the woodland creatures feel the need for more seclusion than their relatives that live in your garden, or it may be that they just happened to be born in the woods and roamed only far enough away from their nursery homes to stake out territories of their own. Each creature has to find a way of life suitable to its needs, with plenty of food and shelter, or it will perish.

As you go toward the woods, see how many animals you can find along the way. Insects swarm up from a bush you brush against. A flock of birds passes overhead on the way to roost for the night, or perhaps they are using the night hours for traveling because they cannot see to hunt food. When you approach the pond, the frog chorus becomes silent as each little peeper slips into the water, although, after you pass, they will all climb out and the music will start again. And be careful not to step on a hollow in the ground, for it may be a rabbit nursery or a nest full of little colored bird's eggs!

12

2

Night in the Woods

The woods at night are not as silent as you might think. The slender green tree cricket begins its song at sundown with a low, purring sound. Soon, thousands have joined in the chorus, all keeping time with about one hundred notes a minute. The whole forest seems to vibrate with this musical concert when you approach it at dusk. Other winged creatures are among the trees and often they too make themselves heard. The whip-poor-will is seldom seen but often heard, repeating the sound of its name, resting only for a moment and continuing from dusk till dawn. This bird flies low, catching insects such as moths, mosquitoes, grasshoppers and the like. The animals of the woods are accustomed to its call and are not alarmed by it.

Sometimes the drumming made by the male ruffed grouse, also known as a partridge, fills the night air. Both the ruffed grouse and the whip-poor-will nest on the woodland floor.

The owls add their weird cries. All of these are not alike. The tiny saw-whet owl endlessly repeats its *too-too-too* over a hundred times a minute. The screech owl, a small red-brown owl with ear tufts, has a mournful wail. The long-eared owl, with ears close together near the center of the forehead, frequents the evergreen woods and its hoot scares all the little woodland animals.

Be sure to take a flashlight along when you walk in the woods at night, for, just as your car headlights are reflected by the eyes of animals along the roadside, your torchlight will be reflected by small eyes in the black shadows of the woods. A pair of tiny, golden, red gleams may be those of a moth resting on a tree trunk; a minute reddish glow may guide you to a wolf spider, searching for insects on the forest floor. A pair of bright yellow, larger spots may be the eyes of a raccoon, quietly waiting for you to pass. The eyes of a bobcat glow a greenish white, just like those of your kitten.

Turn off your light and all the bright spots vanish completely, for they are but "eye shine"—a light reflected from the back of the eye, as the moon reflects the light of the sun. If you wish to see anything more than just eyes silently watching you from the shadows, you must stay in the dark yourself, long enough for your own eyes to become adjusted to night seeing. Then the pupils of your eyes will become large and you will see much better, almost as well as the night-hunting animals. It may take half an hour before you are fully accustomed to the darkness. Then you will have no difficulty in recognizing objects around you.

As you sit quietly on a tree stump, you seem to be part of the forest itself. Perhaps all about you the little flying squirrels are turning the woodland into a playground. When they spread their legs wide apart, the skin between stretches like the wings of a glider and they are able to sail through the air for a hundred feet or more. With a twist of the body or a lift of the tail, the agile animal controls the direction of flight. Don't move or you will frighten away the timid creatures you came to see.

A saw-whet owl turns its head all the way around to watch you.

THE RACCOON

Where the fields and the forest meet, where moonbeams break through the trees, making lacy shadows on the ground below, and a creek winds like a silver ribbon through a deep ravine, you will find the home of the raccoon, the "rogue in a black mask." You may find its den in the crotch of a hollow tree, or in an abandoned muskrat house by the side of the creek, or in a crevice in a rock ledge. Perhaps this small relative of the bear lives in a tree den that has known generations of raccoons.

On a moonlight night, you may watch a mother raccoon take her four month-old babies on their first hunting trip. All the youngsters wear black masks like their mother and also have bushy, black-ringed tails like hers. Their grizzled coats of gray, brown and black fur are soft and thick. The little ones stay near the den on their first trip out into the world, smelling around and examining with their little "hands" every leaf and stump, while their mother sits in the moonlight, watching over them. When at last they grow tired and hungry, they cry in high-pitched voices and the mother sits back on her haunches so they can nurse. The cries cease and the only sound is a soft purring as they become satisfied.

Every night after dusk the mother raccoon brings her cubs out from the den in order to teach them the ways of life. They are filled with curiosity and clamber over every fallen tree, poking their noses into every rotten stump in search for grubs, but always following their mother, for this is the way they learn. She teaches them how to hunt mice, to smell where the turtle has laid her eggs and to climb trees to rob birds' nests. She leads them to the best berry patches and fruit trees. They learn they have to be quick to catch a grasshopper.

Raccoons have the kind of teeth that can tear and chew up flesh, but they also eat grain and fruit—as do foxes, wolves and mink. All of these creatures have keen eyes that see well in the dark and noses that pick up the slightest scent—but only the raccoon among them has feet that can be used as hands. The raccoon can feel in the mud for frogs it cannot see or smell, or in water under a rock for crayfish. I think these sensitive "hands" and the intense curiosity a raccoon shows in everything it sees are what makes the little black-masked animal such fun to watch.

Because raccoons like water so much, they often dabble

their food in a stream, as if they were washing it before eating, but, since they do eat a lot of food that is never "washed," this cannot be the real reason. I expect they like to drink water and this is one way to do it.

The young raccoons learn from their mother the meaning of every important sight and sound, particularly those that signify danger. They know the difference between those which are to be feared and those which are to be ignored. The bark of a dog sends the family scuttling back to the safety of the den, if it is not too distant. If their home is too far away, the mother sends her youngsters up a tree. If they don't obey promptly she cuffs them, and if the last one is too slow in climbing, she

The raccoon dabbles its food in the stream.

18

The mother is affectionate but she tolerates no disobedience.

boosts it up and out of sight. She tolerates no foolishness, for her young have much to learn in order to escape their enemies in the woods.

Finally, the young raccoons learn all the tricks their mother knows, such as outsmarting the hounds by walking on fallen trees, on top of walls, or through streams, to break the scent. They soon discover that there are sounds they need not fear, such as the splash made by a frog, or the squeak of a mouse or a shrew. These are good sounds, suggesting food. The call of the whip-poor-will and the cry of the screech owl can be ignored. Danger lies in the silent ones. The moving shadow of the great horned owl is to be feared, while every rock may hide a bobcat or a coyote. All of this is part of their lessons.

The youngsters repeat what their mother does, over and over, until they can do it as well as she. In the fall, you may see her bending down a cornstalk so that her young can eat the sweet, tender ears. Eating during the fall is, in fact, a serious business for raccoons, and they gorge themselves on everything from grasshoppers to wild grapes, for they have to build up a reserve of fat against the cold winter months when food is scarce. By the time winter starts, they are usually so fat they can hardly move, and the nightly excursions become shorter and shorter. Then, when the cold spell comes, they sleep for several days or even weeks at a time, curled up and snuggled together in the den, living on the fat from the food they ate during those moonlight forages. Every so often the raccoons come out to stretch but the cold soon drives them home again to the warmth of the den.

Perhaps you'll find little tracks in the soft earth in the woods or in the sand near an overturned picnic basket, or even in your own back yard, near the garbage can. Examine them carefully. If these tracks look as though they were made by the bare feet of a small baby, then you have had the rogue-in-the-black-mask as a visitor!

THE PORCUPINE

The porcupine lives most of its life up in a tree, day and night, summer and winter, gnawing the bark, for bark is its favorite food. It is a chisel-tooth, like the beaver, using its front teeth to chisel away the bark. These are quite different from the tearing, slashing teeth of flesh eaters or the heavy, grinding teeth of grass chewers.

If you should chance to come across this animal sitting relaxed upon a limb and eating away, you would see a large, dark, furry creature, with small eyes almost buried in the hair of the face, a little blunt nose and a short thick tail covered with sharp quills. Or you might meet a porcupine actually on the ground, waddling slowly along on its short legs, making its way from a spruce to an oak tree for a change in diet. You'd surely think that here is a good meal for a fox or a bobcat, and

A baby porcupine waits patiently while its mother
eats bark in the tree above.

one very easy to catch.

If your dog is with you, you'll see a sudden change in the porcupine the first time the dog barks, however. Sharp quills hidden in the dark fur now stand up all over the porcupine's body, so that the animal looks like an enormous pincushion. It has no need to run away, for any animal would have to be very stupid or awfully hungry to get within reach of that dangerous, threshing tail with its barbed spears.

Porcupines never shoot their quills, as once was believed, but the quills are so lightly attached to the skin that they pull out if the points stick into anything. Each of them is tipped with many tiny hooks, so if a sharp-pointed quill should stick into the nose of a foolish dog, the hooks make it hard to pull it out again. Most animals are wise enough to give the porcupine a wide berth. Only the fisher seems to find the meat worth the trouble and pain of facing those quills.

Early in springtime, a single baby is born to the porcupine mother, in a den inside a hollow log or under a brushpile or, in fact, in any old place that is partly hidden. The baby is born fully equipped with pointed quills, and infancy is very short. After a week of nursing, the mother starts to wean the youngster by feeding it green herbs. Most of the time the young one lies curled up on the ground beneath the tree in which the mother is eating, although the little porcupine already can climb and it isn't long before it follows its mother slowly but sure-footedly to the lower branches, to nibble tender bark and leaves.

Once I saw a porcupine in an oak tree, eating the mistletoe I had come to gather for Christmas. You may find one, perhaps a mother and young, in a berry patch, sniffing every plant, eating leaves and chewing noisily. Do look up into the trees as you walk in the woods. In the evening—or even in the daytime —you are likely to see a porcupine. Sometimes the animal stays in the same tree for weeks—after all, why change when all the food you want is within easy reach?

THE OPOSSUM

The great dinosaur monsters that roamed the earth long, long ago were too big and clumsy to cope with changing conditions and became extinct. But opossum-like animals that were around at the same time have left us their living descendants which are still much like their ancient ancestors. Some people say opossums are dim-witted, but I am not so sure. They have the secret of survival pretty well worked out, and their ability to hunt at night and to eat everything, from roots to beetles and mice, birds and fruit, are two of the reasons why they manage so well. There are several others.

The opossum is about the size of a large cat and has a buff-colored undercoat of coarse fur and an overcoat of long black-tipped guard hairs. Little pink feet protrude below the dark fur on the legs, looking for all the world like tiny hands extending from black lace gloves. The animal appears to stare at the world through its large black eyes. It hears through leaf-shaped, hairless ears. The long slit of a mouth shows many small, sharp teeth. At the other end of the body is a long, rough, somewhat hairless tail, rather like a rat's, that is especially useful when employed as an extra hand or foot or even as a stool to prop its owner up. The creature is shy and solitary and seems to be so relaxed that it never appears to be in a hurry.

All day long the opossum hides in a hole in the ground, or almost anywhere that is out of sight, waiting for night to fall before it emerges. Food is found by smell. When something is discovered that suits its liking, the queer fellow sits propped up by its tail and eats noisily, with open-mouthed chewing and a great smacking of its lips.

After a good meal, the opossum gives itself a leisurely bath, again propped up by its tail, starting with the face, then the neck and body, and finally thoroughly washing the little pink toes. With its grooming completed, it ambles slowly along, maybe to a persimmon tree, and climbs easily, using its long sharp claws and the little suction pads on its toes. Then, wrapping its prehensile tail around a branch for safety's sake, the opossum reaches far out on a limb to take a persimmon, its favorite fruit. If you live where persimmon trees grow, you know exactly where you are most likely to see one of these fellows enjoying a meal.

When a female is about to have her litter of young she is no longer content with any old home but searches out a deserted owl's nest, or even an unoccupied skunk's den, and moves in. The peculiar tail again is useful, for she winds it around bundles of grass and leaves that she takes home for nesting material.

When the babies are born, they are no larger than small

Opossum

A baby opossum looks about at the world after two months in a pouch.

beans. They don't look like very much of anything but each has four tiny nubbins that will grow out into legs. The front pairs already have little claws and these are used for climbing the three inches of fur to the safety and warmth of the mother's pouch, where they continue their development. Once inside the pouch, each baby grasps one of the thirteen nipples and hangs on for dear life. It really is for dear life, for it is a case of first come, first served. Often there are more than thirteen offspring, so that only the first to come can find a nipple to which to attach itself. The mother pumps milk from her nipples into these lucky ones for the next two months.

Another reason why the opossum has survived so long when many of its fellow creatures have failed is the continued care the mother takes of her young. Wherever she goes, she carries her babies with her.

You may see a female with her pouch so full of growing youngsters that it almost drags on the ground. Or you may happen on her after about two months have gone by, when the little opossums, now about the size of mice, have ventured outside to look at the world around them. You may see them clinging to her fur or they may be peering from the safety of the pouch, with only their little white faces showing. They return to the warmth and safety of the pouch, to nurse and sleep, until they are fully weaned and able to take care of themselves. Later on, when their legs are stronger, you may see them toddling beside their mother as they cross a patch of moonlight on the forest floor.

This slow-moving animal seems to have little protection from its enemies, particularly dogs and men. You would think every other creature in the woods would get the better of it; yet, obviously, it must have some means of defense or else opossums should no longer be around. One trick that it has perfected is to play dead. When caught or cornered, the opossum lies limply on its side, with its mouth open. There seems to be no life left at all, but the minute the enemy is no longer watching, the opossum jumps up and runs lickety-split into the woods again. We call this "playing 'possum."

If you live where opossums have their homes, you may already know and like these creatures of the forest. When you hear dogs barking in the woods at night, you will know, as I did when I was your age, that it probably means that an opossum has been cornered up a tree, and, like me, you will hope the little fellow escapes into the night.

THE WHITE-TAILED DEER

Along the edge of the forest, where there is enough sunlight to allow willows, maples and oak trees to thrive, the witch hazel and dogwood form thickets that are just right to protect the white-tailed deer. The sunlight slips between the leaves and

27

The fawn hides in a bed of ferns.

makes a pattern of light and dark on the ferns and blueberry bushes that cover the forest floor.

There, on a bed of ferns, two newborn fawns lie asleep. Their polka-dot, reddish-brown coats serve as good camouflage, for they blend so well with the pattern of sun and shade across the undergrowth that they are almost invisible. Their keen ears hear a tiny twig crack and their heads pop up with the large, round eyes wide awake. Their mother, a graceful doe, steps almost noiselessly into the thicket of dogwood.

The fawns, weighing no more than five pounds each, struggle up on their long, weak legs and take a few wobbly steps to nuzzle their mother, for they are hungry. While they nurse, the doe watches and listens with her head held high for any sign of danger. She had been feeding nearby and keeping an eye on the nursery in the thicket. She dares not go to her twins, to feed them, more often than every couple of hours, for she does not want to call attention to their hiding place.

When the pair are contentedly satisfied, she pushes them gently to the ground and leaves them as quietly as she came. The fawns have no strong scent that might attract enemies, and their spotted coats make them invisible as long as they stay still. After a meal, they sleep for an hour or so, then wake and become restless—maybe a little hungry again or perhaps just stiff and needing to stretch. At any rate, after a little bird-like twittering, they stand up and wander a few feet from the bed of ferns. If a bird flies close, they drop at once to the ground without a sound. Each time the doe returns to feed them they jump up again, and each time their legs are just a little bit stronger.

The mother often has to wander out of hearing distance to find food for herself, for she needs to eat a lot while nursing her twins. A deer has no means of storing food near her young, nor could she very well carry it, even if she had. She can only eat and eat, for those twins need a great deal of milk. But she knows that if a fox, coyote or bobcat happened to find the nursery in the thicket, it would kill her babies, so she doesn't go far afield. When she returns, she stands for a long time, sniffing the air and listening, before she dares go near their hiding place. If all seems well, she approaches silently, and when her young have again been fed, she as silently departs.

When the twin fawns are about four weeks old they are strong enough to travel with their mother, and on some warm evening they follow her out of the thicket and along a forest trail to a pond where water lilies grow. There they wade into

The doe approaches the thicket silently, to feed her twins.

the cool water and eat the lily leaves and other pond weeds. Here, a breeze blows the insects away, which is a welcome relief after the long weeks in the thicket. The pair discover they can swim to reach the lily pads further away from shore. Each night thereafter, throughout the summer, the doe and her fawns go to the pond. Sometimes they stop to play and run about in a forest meadow, but any strange noise brings the doe's white tail up in warning and the fawns run with her to the shelter of the thick forest.

Sometimes, on their nightly travels, they see a deer with great horns. These are the bucks which have spent the summer growing antlers. When they do meet a buck, the doe and her fawns turn off the trail, into the denser woods.

By August, the bucks' antlers are full grown and have begun to itch so much that the animals rub them against the trunks and branches of trees, to scrape off the "velvet" covering of skin. You may find pieces of dried skin hanging on the side of a tree trunk and know therefore that a male deer has freed his antlers and is ready to fight other bucks for the attention of some beautiful doe. And in the fall, you may hear antlers clashing sharply as the bucks charge one another. But I am sure you will never have a greater thrill than when you see a graceful doe, followed by her fawns, step out of a thicket into the moonlight and walk silently along a forest trail.

THE JUMPING MOUSE

The champion jumper of the world is a tiny mouse which makes ten-foot leaps to escape an enemy. As a rule, the little jumper travels in a zigzag manner, taking long, four- to six-foot jumps above the woodland grass. The tail, longer than the head and body together, is used as a balancer. On landing, the mouse "freezes" for a long time, for safety's sake—no scampering through the grass to let the owl know where to find it. The

yellow-brown coat with blackish hairs over the back makes the animal almost invisible among the grass stems, even in daylight.

The jumping mouse is nervous and high-strung, like most of its relatives, and needs much food to supply its energy. Each night, the mouse eats half its own weight in seeds, spruce needles, tender shoots and other plants, as well as moths, flies and any other insects it can catch. The creature will run up a stem to bend the flower or seeds over to the ground where, sitting up, it strips the plant, using its forepaws as hands.

After feeding, the clean little animal washes its white vest and golden-brown coat by licking every hair. Then it jumps away, like a small kangaroo, to its globe-shaped nest of grass and leaves. The four-inch-wide nest is usually on the ground and resembles the vegetation around it, but sometimes it is raised a few inches off the ground, suspended by grass stems. One kind of jumping mouse even digs tunnels underground.

When winter comes, the jumping mouse is so fat from all the food it has eaten that it can hardly walk, much less jump, so it goes into an underground home, below the frost line, rolls into a ball and sleeps through the cold winter.

If you want to see the woodland jumping mouse during the summer, look near forest streams, for water is very necessary to this little animal. Maybe you'll see its white tail-brush as it disappears with a long, high jump into the darkness. (Another kind of jumping mouse lives in damp meadows and has a black-tipped tail.)

The jumping mouse utters a deep note, not at all like the usual squeak of a mouse, and sometimes it drums on the ground with its long tail. These are the ways by which it communicates with all the other jumping mice in the woods nearby.

The fox parents watch carefully over their pups.

THE RED FOX

The red fox, about the size of a small collie dog, walks cautiously from the dark shadows of the woods into the open space beyond, with eyes alert for any movement in the tall grass ahead and ears erect, listening intently. Lifting each leg high, the fox comes into view, and we see the golden-reddish coat, colorful even in the moonlight. The fur is long and the tail bushy, and its black legs and feet make the animal appear to be wearing long black stockings.

33

A red fox is brave enough to venture into the open, well outside the deep woods, for a little hunting. It will even tackle a young deer but is usually satisfied with mice and rabbits. Sometimes the red hunter stalks its prey and pounces, much as a cat does. At other times, the animal steps high and slowly through the long grass, eating crickets and other insects. Or the fellow may go to a berry patch or stop in an orchard, beneath an apple tree, feeding on the fallen apples. The fox knows when the wild grapes are ripe, as well as where the turtle lays her eggs. When it makes a kill too big to be eaten all at once, it carefully covers the remains with leaves or snow, according to the season, and returns later for another meal.

In the distance, a dog barks but the fox continues serenely on its way. The fox hears but is not afraid, for, although a dog may be stronger, the fox can outwit it almost every time. All the tricks concerning how to shake off an enemy have been well learned and practiced, such as walking on logs and in streams to break the scent trail, the way the raccoon does, or just circling around and coming up behind a pack of hounds. The fox seems to enjoy matching wits with the dog—and, as for its other enemies, such as the coyote, wolf and bobcat, only a weak or foolish fox is in any danger of being caught. The fox we watch finally disappears into the woods again and we realize we have seen a creature of rare intelligence, beautiful in both color and grace.

3

Night in the Deep Forest

In the deep forest, where the tall trees meet overhead, allowing little sun to reach the shadowy floor, and the underbrush grows too thick to penetrate, many animals live their private lives, some rarely if ever seen. If you could discover a trail and walk along it some evening when all is dark, you would probably be surprised to find the pathway gleaming with a strange light produced by fungi growing along the way. A rotten log gives off an eerie greenish glow, made by the minute bacteria growing in the soft, decaying wood. This is called "fox fire." There is nothing more startling than to see an owl, whose feathers have rubbed against some decaying logs, swoop silently past, like a greenish-white glowing ghost.

THE WOOD RAT

Many shy creatures prefer to live in the heavy undergrowth of the dense woods and come out only at night, when darkness hides all that is strange or dangerous. The wood rat is one of these and any woodland camper will come across its home under a pile of debris and sticks. This gentle little animal's

habit of collecting objects—feathers, pebbles, shells, any bright thing—has given it the name of "pack rat." More than one camper or lumberman has wakened to find his watch missing and a shiny stone left in its place. This sort of thing has given rise to the idea that the pack rat is no robber but a trader who always leaves something in exchange for what has been taken away. Actually, the animal is fascinated by anything bright, so drops what it already carries, picks up the newest bright object and scurries home with it.

Never confuse this attractive, intelligent and clean little animal with its relatives, the dirty city rats, for they have little in common. The pack rat, however, does not live only in the forest, for it is equally at home on the plains and in the desert. It knows how to get along wherever it is.

Overhead in the deep woods sits the great horned owl, one of the most majestic of the owls. Its brown coat with black and grey mottling makes it difficult to see, but its *hoo-hoo*, often repeated, strikes fear into the hearts of the wood rat and all the other small creatures within hearing.

THE SNOWSHOE HARE

The snowshoe hare chooses to live in the big woods where there is plenty of undergrowth for protection and so rarely ventures out into open country. As a matter of fact, it remains within a mile of its home all its life. To a hare, home is a "form," a hollow place made by the weight of its body in the leafy floor of the woods. Usually it is situated on a slight knoll—the better to see approaching enemies—or else it is hidden in tall shrubs. The animal sits huddled, with its head, neck and body drawn close together and with its long ears held high and continually turning about to catch every sound. Several of these "forms" are scattered over its home territory, and the hare may be sitting quietly in any one of them, always on the alert.

The snowshoe hare is also called the varying hare and the two names describe it well. The summer coat of brown and white is in winter changed to a pure white coat, with only the dark eyes and black-tipped ears to show where it sits in the snow. This changeable coloring is why the animal has been given its second name.

All hares have larger ears and legs than rabbits, and the snowshoe hare has especially long and strong legs, so large that they are used like snowshoes for traveling over the top of the snow during the winter—hence its first name. By means of these strong legs, the animal can go straight from a sitting position into a fast run that quickly speeds up to thirty or forty miles an hour. The springs achieved by the powerful hind legs can take the hare twelve feet with every jump, making it about the fastest creature in the forest.

The snowshoe hare spends the first and the last hours of darkness feeding on grasses and shrubs. Much of the time between is spent combing its fur coat with the long claws of its

In winter dress the snowshoe hare is almost invisible.

hind feet and washing its face with its paws, as cats do. On moonlight nights, several hares are sometimes seen sitting close together in a circle in a forest clearing. Any noise sends each to its own form, where it sits motionless, blending with the background. The hares know their well-traveled trails and are familiar with every hiding place in their territory.

Young hares are born wherever the mother happens to be when the time comes, and usually there are three to five babies. They are fully covered with fine brown hair right from the start, and have their eyes open. (Cottontail babies are born naked and blind.) The mother hare visits the young to feed them only at night. During the daylight hours she remains nearby to watch over them. If a bobcat, coyote, wolf, fox or weasel comes too close, she leads it far away on a merry chase, for she can outrun them all. She usually then shelters in a hollow log or the burrow of a skunk until the enemy leaves and she can return to her family.

From the very first the baby hares can hop about. After a couple of weeks you may see them nibbling grass in the moonlight. They are well concealed as long as they remain still, but one slight noise may bring the great horned owl swooping down on them.

On occasion the snowshoe hare thumps with its big hind feet, making a sound that can be heard far through the forest. Why it does so is still one of nature's mysteries.

THE GREAT HORNED OWL

The first large egg of the horned owl is laid in February, in a nest in one of the tallest trees in the forest. Sometimes the nest is a discarded one of a crow or even an eagle. The female begins to brood right away because, in some parts of the world, the temperature may be below zero at this time of year and the eggs must be kept warm all the time if they are to hatch. She lays a second egg a few days later and often a third. She sits on the eggs for a full month while her mate roosts on a nearby limb of the tree all day and hunts all night for food. Usually, he brings his mate food at dusk but sometimes she slips silently away from the nest for a short hunting trip on her own.

She returns just as silently and lands nearby on a branch, then hops carefully to the nest. She always goes through the same ritual of turning over the eggs with her beak and rubbing her face slowly around each egg. When the "nuzzling" is over, she moves closer above the eggs and pushes them carefully, one by one, into her breast feathers until they are entirely covered by her brood pouch.

When a month has passed, the first egg hatches into a white, downy owl chick, blind and helpless. A few days later the second egg hatches. By this time the earlier chick has grown considerably. From the first there is no mistaking them for anything but baby owls. All day the downy chicks sit up high in their nest and look about them and preen their feathers. At dusk they become restless and hungry and tell their parents about it in no uncertain terms! The parents, who have spent the day roosting on a nearby branch, now swoop silently into the deep woods and their hooting calls are heard as they hunt. Occasionally, a parent answers the call of the young birds with a note quite different from the hooting sound. Excitement in the nest grows as the owlets become more and more hungry. A branch cracks as one of the parents lands near the nest with food in its talons. When the young have been sufficiently fed with choice bits of meat, they become satisfied and silent, and once more the hoots of the parents are heard as they hunt again in the deep forest, this time for food for themselves.

The great horned owl, with a wing spread as wide as a man is tall, is able to fly without making any noise at all because of the soft feathers that muffle the sound of the beating wings completely. They swoop silently down to strike at the spot where the sound of some scurrying animal was last heard. The great, round eyes of the bird are used to avoid flying into tree branches, but the extraordinary ears, used for hunting, are the keenest in the bird world. The feathers of the face are curved

40

in such a way that they collect even the slightest sound.

When their wing feathers are well developed, the owlets climb about on the branches near the nest. In their eagerness to be fed, they almost knock the parent off the nest when one lands with food clutched in its talons. Soon they are big enough to fly out into the dark every night, to capture their own food and add their own hooting calls to the sounds of the shadowy forest.

THE GRAY FOX

The gray fox, which is smaller and much shyer than the red fox, prefers the denser woods and thickets, where it can quickly climb a tree if attacked, or hide in the thick foilage. Sometimes even in the daytime, you may see one of these handsome little fellows lying across a tree limb, resting in the sunlight.

In the spring, the fat young foxes of each family play on their "doorstep," wrestling and rolling and tumbling about like lively puppies. Their parents had previously selected an abandoned

underground den of some other animal, cleaned it out and temporarily moved in. The babies were born here and the father, an excellent provider, brought food to his mate so that she need not leave her offspring unguarded. The whole family remains here while the youngsters play and grow strong, with one or both parents constantly watching the sky with their sharp eyes for a threatening owl or an eagle.

By late summer the young foxes, each wearing a soft gray coat with a black stripe from the neck to the tip of the tail, leave the nursery to accompany their parents, hunting by day and night. They sleep where they happen to be when rest is needed, all curled up with their beautiful tails covering their feet and noses.

Their hunting lessons continue and they learn to twist and leap with quickness and grace, their tails held high for balance, while they endeavor to catch mice and rabbits. They never store food, as their red-coated relatives do, but eat immediately all that they kill.

BOBCATS

This wild relative of your pet cat hunts at night and just about everywhere from the cold north to the hot desert—that is, wherever there are trees, underbrush, or rock crevices in which to hide and open ground on which to hunt the small animals that make up its food.

The bobcat may hide on a tree limb for, like your cat, the wild one is a good climber, or it may hide behind a rock or a bush, ready to spring out if a woodchuck or muskrat passes. This cat is so silent and blends so well with the night shadows that I am sure you would not be able to see it. The spotted coat and short, ringed tail is apt to be dark in animals that hunt

in the deep, dark woods, and pale in those that live in the desert. The young kits are very spotted, whereas the older cats have a plainer coat. And in cold climates the bobcat's coat is thick and heavy, but it is lightweight in warmer places.

Each wildcat has a home range of about five square miles—too much to cover in a single night, of course, although any night's hunting may take the creature several miles from home.

The bobcat, which weighs from fifteen to forty pounds, hunts by sight rather than by smell, for it has special eyes, like your cat's, which can make use of even the dimmest light. It can stalk cottontails and snowshoe rabbits on the darkest nights, when only the stars are gleaming. With its keen eyes, the cat studies every shadow before moving forward, and it can detect the slightest stir on the ground or in the trees. Then it creeps ahead on silent feet—close enough to leap at an unsuspecting rabbit. Often the wild cat lies waiting, flattened to the ground—just as your kitten does—watching a runway, ready to spring on the first shy mouse that ventures too close. If the mouse is running fast, the spring of the cat is aimed well ahead of it and there is little chance of escape. If the bobcat should miss, however, it doesn't give chase but waits for another small animal to come along.

Although the wild cats are silent hunters, when it comes time for courting, their screaming and howling serenades can be heard for miles through the quiet night air. They sound just like the fighting of city alley cats, except that they are much louder and carry much farther.

You may never see a wild cat in the forest but one may be watching you. Have no fear, it will slink away unseen, for it doesn't want to meet you—although you may get a funny feeling at the back of your head that someone is watching you. However, a bobcat cornered will fight savagely—wild cat that it is! It screams, spits and scratches, again just like your own cat, which hasn't changed so much, after all, from its wild relative, has it?

If dawn finds the bobcat far from home, it selects a place out

45

of sight to sleep through the sunlit hours.

Perhaps some day you'll see deep scratches on a dead tree trunk and you will know at once that a bobcat has been sharpening its claws there. You'll recognize them because they are so much like the ones your kitten makes on a chair at home—but larger, and deeper, of course.

THE MARTEN AND THE FISHER

When you see little red squirrels scrambling to their treetop homes at sunset, and birds flying to their nests or roosting places, I expect you think, "Now they are safe—all tucked away for the night." But this isn't always true, for there are hunters that spend most of their nights in the treetops, too, hunting for what they can find. The marten is one of these.

Like all weasels, the marten is quick, intelligent and strong, with sharp teeth and claws. It is wild and savage and can out-leap any squirrel as it dashes about among the branches in the spruce and balsam fir forests, always on the hunt by night and day. The red squirrel is safe only if it can reach a hole in a hollow tree that is too small for this oversized weasel to enter.

Sometimes the marten travels for miles through the treetops without coming down to earth. Hunger may bring it to the floor of the forest, where the woodchuck, shrew, wood rat and other small animals have little chance to escape.

There is another weasel, the fisher, that is even larger and darker than the marten and can outwit it. Strange to say, in spite of its name, it doesn't fish but hunts in the treetops like the marten and is so fast and strong that it has little to fear from any other animal.

The fisher is about the size of a fox and has a fluffy tail like the fox, but its face is weasel-like and it jumps about on short legs,

46

The marten travels about in the treetops.

just like its smaller weasel relatives which you may have seen in your back yard. The creature is a good climber and spends most of the night hunting animals that live in the trees. It also hunts on the ground and eats or stores for a future meal everything it desires, whether it be squirrel, rabbit, rat, beaver, fox or raccoon—and even the marten, for it is swifter and more powerful

The fisher is a good climber as well as an efficient hunter.

than most animals it hunts. In fact the fisher is almost the only creature known that can eat a porcupine without suffering any ill consequences!

These two giant weasels, the marten and the fisher, are flesh eaters and hunt only for food, never for sport. They are efficient, quick and intelligent. We must admire them for these characteristics, even if they are the enemies of the more familiar animals we know and like. The forest world is made up of all kinds of creatures and, at night, each according to his nature must find food in order to live. Yes, the marten and the fisher are savage and wild. We could never make pets of them—but neither have we any need to, fortunately!

THE WOLF

From the very first time we are told nursery stories we hear of the "Big, Bad Wolf" which is either "huffing and puffing" to blow the house down or baring his long, sharp teeth, "the better to eat you with." It is time now that you heard a little of the other side of the story, for, actually, the wolf is a most admirable character.

The wolf is kind and devoted to his mate, whom he "marries for life." No father was ever more gentle and tender to his young or more conscientious as a family provider of food, or a more patient teacher of woodland skills—but enough of this. You must see just how wolves really live and then judge them for yourself.

A female gray wolf pokes her long, slender nose into an underground burrow and sniffs. The smell of badger is there but too faint for the occupant to be still present, so the wolf disappears inside. Her mate follows, and, almost at once, they begin to remodel the den, for the bedroom is not large enough for a wolf nursery. A leisurely survey shows that the entrance is too unprotected and a badger could easily force the doorway and reach young baby wolves. So the female sniffs around the base of a tree and starts to dig. When she has finished, a new tunnel leads to the nursery, with the new entrance now between two large roots. The old entrance is then closed up and the pair of wolves move in.

The wolf finds the going hard in the deep snow.

49

Later, on the bare earth of the den, six (there can be as many as fourteen!) grayish-brown, fluffy-coated cubs are born. Their mother stays with them all the time, except when she goes to the entrance to eat the meat her mate has brought for her. His job is a hard one, for he dare not go far away from his precious family and so must hunt nearby, mainly for "small stuff," such as rabbits, squirrels and the like.

The wolf is a social animal and lives in a co-operative family group called a "pack." The aunts and uncles and all the children of all the past two or three years help by bringing food to the den entrance of the nursing mother.

The cubs open their eyes when they are about one week old, although there is little to see in the dark nursery below the ground. After three weeks, the mother begins to wean them on partly digested food she "spits up." Remember, these baby wolves will be meat eaters but, until they have teeth strong enough to chew raw meat, their mother must meet their needs in her own way. Your own mother bought, cooked and strained food when you needed more than milk and still had no teeth with which to chew.

The cubs play in the sun at the entrance to the den, with at least one of them on the lookout for a bobcat or an owl or even a bear that might like a tasty wolf cub for dinner! By this time, of course, the entrance is in no way disguised, for there is a well-beaten path to the door.

The wolf family had taken only a temporary lease on its home for nursery purposes. After two months have gone by, the cubs can chew meat and are strong enough to accompany their parents on the nightly hunt. At first they travel slowly and their hunting trips are short, but they soon become big enough to keep up with the pack.

The parents stay close to their cubs, to guard and to teach them first of all how to catch mice, gophers and rabbits. The

50

A wolf cub sits in the sun at the entrance to the den.

cubs watch eagerly and imitate everything that their parents do. They learn to run after a herd of deer until a weak or crippled animal falls behind, and then how to make a quick kill. If food is scarce, they cover part of their catch and return to it when they are hungry again. If plentiful, the wolves eat what they want and leave the rest for the foxes or bears which are always looking for the leavings of the wolf packs. Finally, the cubs become trained in the relay system of hunting, where a part of the pack runs after a herd while fresh runners wait ahead to take over when the first pursuers are tired.

You may hear the long low howl of a wolf in the night. This doesn't mean that the members of a pack are having a fight, for they never snap at one another. This family sociability and co-operation is just another of the admirable qualities of the handsome wolf.

The hunting range of the wolf pack may extend one hundred miles, and often this distance is covered several times each month. Wolves hunt in order to live. It's a pity that they can make no distinction between a farmer's animals and the wild ones. It is only because of this unhappy failure to leave domestic animals alone that the story of the "Big Bad Wolf" grew, and so the wolf was and still is killed as man's number one wild enemy.

When this country was covered with dense forests, the wolf knew it from coast to coast. Because it killed only the weaker animals, the herds of deer remained strong and vigorous and nature was kept in balance. Man kills those animals with the largest antlers, the best of the herd, and has long since killed off most of the wolves. He has upset this balance of nature, and the wolf, the most intelligent and humane member of the wild community, has disappeared from most of the great forests, perhaps forever.

THE BLACK BEAR

A mother bear is very secretive and likes to keep her twin cubs well hidden, so she chooses a shady spot in the dense bushes and settles down to nurse them. The cubs were born when she was still in her winter sleep in her den and were already three months old when spring came. Only then did she bring her twins out to learn the ways of the world. And you have never seen a more devoted mother—no creature will fight more fiercely if its young are attacked.

One of the first lessons the mother bear teaches her cubs is how to use their sharp claws for climbing to the treetops where they can find safety quickly. When she sends them up, she means it, and any hesitation calls for a slap from a heavy paw. All mothers of the wild demand obedience and the bear—one of the most affectionate mothers—is one of the strictest.

For a whole year her time is given to her cubs for she alone cares for them. She teaches them how to rob a bee's nest of its honey, just which stumps are filled with grubs and ants and where tender roots grow. She takes them to the stream to show them how to use their paws to slap fish out onto the shore. They learn which trees are unsafe to climb because of rotten wood. She plays with her cubs and they scramble all over her and tease her; when she gets tired of this, she orders them up a tree while she rests below. She is affectionate and tender with her twins and cuddles them in her arms at times, and at night they all bed down together in a thicket, wherever they may be. You may even come across a place where the grass and shrubs have been flattened and know that a bear and her cubs slept there.

THE MOOSE

A moose feeding at night, especially a large bull, can be heard a mile away. A loud slap means that the broad, heavy antlers have been plunged under water as the animal reaches for duckweed growing on the bottom of a shallow lake. When he raises his head again for air, the sound of the water rushing off the antlers is like a waterfall. He snorts and puffs and plunges down again.

The moose, with the largest antlers of any living animal, spreading more than six feet across, may weigh over a thousand pounds; yet it can disappear into the dark forest as silently as

The moose wades into the stream in search of water plants.

a snowshoe hare. It doesn't travel far afield but spends its life within a somewhat small area, feeding day and night. Sometimes a moose kneels down to eat grasses and sedges, but usually, in the forest, the animal stands on its hind legs and reaches twelve feet up to tear leaves from such trees as the willow, birch, ash and cottonwood. In the woods you may come across this great humped-shouldered creature at any time, day or night, drowsing away while standing and chewing its cud.

Each spring the cow moose has her buff-colored calf—usually only one. The baby has a black muzzle, a black spot over each eye, a bell of loose skin at the neck, but no hump. There are no spots to camouflage it as it hides in the woods. The mother, however, is alert and keeps her large ears in constant motion as she listens and sniffs the air with wide-flared nostrils for possible danger to her calf.

After a week or so, the calf's long legs are strong enough for it to travel with its mother, and for the whole of the following year they are never separated. They wander along the streams and woodland lakes, eating grass and shrubs. Sometimes, they swim out to a lush growth of water plants. When the calf becomes tired, it rests with its neck across the mother's back and she brings her youngster safely to the shore. In the water, they also find relief from the insects that plague them. Often they roll in the mud by the edge of a stream. Being covered with mud may discourage the bugs but it certainly doesn't add to the moose's beauty!

The mating call of a cow moose travels far in the quiet of the forest night. Bulls within hearing answer the call and often the autumn quiet is broken by the sound of fighting as two rivals crash through the undergrowth, swinging their antlers furiously. Hides are slashed and antlers broken. Finally, one gives up and backs away into the darkness.

You may find a place in the great woods where the ground is all torn up and the trees and shrubs trampled down. If so, you will know you missed watching a good fight. Perhaps some day you will see one of these greatest of all antlered creatures, although when he catches sight of you he will move swiftly away, with scarcely a sound, into the depths of the forest.

4

Night on the Desert and Plains

The tall cactus plants cast weird shadows across the desert sands. Grass and wild oats grow sparingly among poppy and lupine. Scattered between the low shrubs there are four-foot-high mounds of sand, dotting the landscape as far as you can see. Some of them measure as much as fifteen feet across. On a dark night, when you turn your flashlight onto one of these, you will see little red eyes peering out at you from the entrance to a tunnel. Listen quietly and you may hear a light thumping noise—a warning to you from the small occupant, sounded by its long hind feet. Turn off your light and wait awhile. If it is not too dark, you'll be surprised to see the little animal leap into the air and land five feet away from its home.

This is the kangaroo rat—not really a kangaroo at all, although it jumps like one, using its oversized hind legs for springing. In fact, the animal is not even a rat, its closest relative being the pocket mouse. Both creatures possess fur-lined shoulder pockets in which to carry food home. The kangaroo rat, which measures about a foot from its nose to the end of its brush-tipped tail, is buff colored and consequently blends with the sand. Its forefeet are tiny and are used as hands rather than feet, while the tail, longer than the head and body together, acts as a balancer in the great jumps and serves as one of the supports when the animal makes a three-point landing.

The timid creature hops about, eating seeds and stuffing grass, which it has cut in short lengths, into its shoulder pockets, using its "hands" that move so fast they can hardly be seen. The little fellow keeps sniffing the air for the smell of badger. Its small ears are forever listening for the sound of a coyote, fox or bobcat, and its alert black eyes endlessly watch the sky for hawk and owl. When, suddenly, there is a whir of wings, the kangaroo rat shows what it can do in an emergency. It leaps ten feet or more to one of the entrance holes to its burrow and disappears underground until the enemy leaves.

Soon, there are many kangaroo rats jumping about close by. When they are feeding each leap is only about a foot long, but when in a hurry they cover fourteen feet with every jump, with their tails twisting about to keep them in balance. Each time they land, the tail comes down with a whack on the hard-packed ground.

All kinds of seeds are gathered for eating and storing, as well as grasses and the leaves of shrubs. It is quite a sight to watch a kangaroo rat jumping about, trying to catch beetles and grasshoppers to add to its diet. When thirsty the small creature simply sips dew.

With its fur-lined pockets filled, the little animal returns to the home mound to deposit the harvested grain in the. storeroom. The mound that shows above ground is made by the accumulation from the diggings that go on down below, as well as husks and droppings—a result of house cleaning. Several entrances are made in the family mound, high enough to keep flood waters from entering the burrows. Underneath there is a system of tunnels that branches in every direction. Our kangaroo rat empties its pockets into one of the storage rooms along the passage and, taking six-inch hops, continues to the bedroom at the very bottom of the tunnel. There, in a circular room, ten inches across, the animal curls up for a rest on a soft bed of grass. Every night, after an hour of feeding and gleaning, it takes a rest, then starts to remodel its home. For a while the dirt flies in all directions as the strong hind feet dig away. Before daylight there is another foraging trip for food.

Just before dawn the kangaroo rat takes a bath, although in its own special way, without water. Because the desert air is so dry, the hair must be kept oiled. The little fellow sits on top of the family mound and, with its paws, distributes oil, collected from glands located on the shoulders, all through its fur. As a final touch, like a dry shampoo, the animal rolls in the dust to remove any extra oil—and the bath is completed.

There is always a fight when a kangaroo rat returns home to find its cousin, the Marrian kangaroo rat, stealing from its storehouse. The Marrian kangaroo rats live in colonies with no thought of the future. They depend entirely on thieving from their thrifty relatives, even though one kick from the strong jumping legs of the kangaroo rat can break the back of an intruder.

59

The same powerful legs are a godsend when the small creature is twisting and turning to avoid being captured by a coyote or bobcat while heading for home. If the enemy is a badger there is less chance for escape, for the badger excavates the mound with great digging claws. If the kangaroo rat is in its tunnel, it often manages to break through the wall and escape, however. Snakes, which can crawl into any entrance hole, are even harder to get away from safely.

During the daytime, the little jumpers are all in their homes, protected from the heat of the desert sun which may raise the temperature on the surface to 150 degrees. You could fry an egg on the hot sand and rocks and, of course, these animals could not stand such heat. Underground, where it is cool, they can comfortably sleep the hot hours away.

THE POCKET MOUSE

When twilight comes and the daytime hunters have gone to roost, the shy pocket mouse breaks down the door of its burrow and scurries out in search of nourishment. It is afraid to travel far and finds its food as close to home as possible. It eats seeds, grass, wild mustard, juniper berries and tender leaves, and, if you watch closely, you can see the small "hands" quickly pack seeds into the fur-lined pocket at each side of its neck, to take home to its underground burrow. Such stores come in very handy during a long drought, when everything has dried up, or on rainy nights, when everything is too wet.

The pocket mouse, a close relative of the kangaroo rat, may have a mound for its home, or the entrance to its burrow may be just a hole in the desert floor, but there is always a storeroom and a small bedroom. The burrow and rooms need not be large, for the animal weighs but one third of an ounce. One thing is

60

certain, when this tiny fellow has finished the nightly food gathering and returns home, it carefully plugs up the entrance to its burrow for added protection.

This gentle pocket mouse is pursued by the coyote, fox, badger, skunk and every other night-hunting animal of the deserts and plains, and by owls as well. No wonder the small creature moves so quickly from shadow to shadow and eats so fast. Pocket mice must be scared all the time they are not curled up on their seed-shuck beds below ground, with their burrow entrances tightly closed.

THE GROUND SQUIRREL

The ground squirrel receives its name from living underground rather than in the trees, as its red and gray relatives do. There are few trees on the prairies and deserts, so only below ground offers any protection against either the hot sun or pursuing animals such as the coyote and fox—although not from the badger.

The striped ground squirrel has thirteen light and dark stripes on its buff-colored back. The dark brown stripes are outlined with spots forming dotted lines. This little squirrel

spends half of the year feeding on grains, grasses, mice and grasshoppers, until it becomes very fat. Then it curls up underground on a bed of soft grass to sleep through the other half of the year.

The ground squirrels are never safe when they are running about at night, but many animals of the plains and deserts would go hungry if there were not so many little squirrels around, flicking their tails and darting in and out of burrows.

THE WHITE-THROATED WOOD RAT

The white-throated wood rat lives on the plains and deserts, as well as in the woods from which it gets its name, but it doesn't burrow like its neighbors, the kangaroo rat, pocket mouse and ground squirrel. To escape the desert heat, it builds a fortress of sharp cactus spines, which may stand five feet high.

The nest is near the center of the pile, close to the ground. It is made of shredded grasses and cactus. The entrance runways are lined with cactus joints, with the spines pointing upward. It is a wonder that the animal doesn't injure its own tender feet going in and out of the nest, and more of a wonder that a cactus spine doesn't pierce its small body when the home is being built.

Once inside their "barbed-wire" fortress, the wood rats are safe from their various enemies, the coyotes, bobcats, owls and skunks. All day long they sleep through the 150-degree desert heat, beneath the insulation of the cactus, and it is there that their young are born and raised. But at night, when they go out for food, they are unprotected. Only their ability to reach the security of their homes saves them if they are attacked. Once they get back inside, they are safe, however, for few animals are crazy enough to try to enter their spiky house—even the badger knows better!

Wood rats are lovely little creatures, not at all like our city rats. Actually, they look like a larger copy of the white-footed mouse, with soft, clean, glossy fur, long whiskers that twitch constantly, and alert black eyes.

THE BADGERS

Badgers live where the soil is sandy and digging is easy, which means there are many badgers in prairie and desert country to keep the small, burrowing animals in a state of constant terror. This rather large animal, about two feet long, with powerful paws and long, sharp claws, can out-dig any other animal. Ground squirrels and kangaroo rats hiding in their underground homes are easily reached in a short time.

If the badger is in danger of attack, it can perform a disappearing act unequaled by any other creature. Employing all

63

four feet—and mouth as well—the animal makes the soft sand
fly in all directions. In a matter of seconds even the tail vanishes
and the hole is plugged from below. Nothing shows where the
animal was except newly dug sand or soft earth. When it has
to, the badger can and does fight fiercely. Dogs have trouble
getting a grip because of its thick fur and loose skin, and the
sharp claws can do much damage. The badger can also give
off a smell of musk, somewhat like a skunk, which may warn
off other animals.

A badger is a heavy, tough creature, with long, shaggy, silver-
gray, grizzled hair and short, bowed legs. Since the claws also
turn in, we can even say the animal is pigeon-toed! Because
the claws are so important in digging for food and in defense,
the badger takes good care of its nails. Sometimes one will sit
by the entrance to its burrow, busily cleaning all the dirt from

between its toes.

The badger is unsociable and always hunts alone, except when a mother is with her young, perhaps teaching them to dig for pocket mice and other small animals. Sometimes the cubs play and romp in an open space near their burrow.

Most of a badger's life seems to be spent hunting for food. It is small wonder that the shy creatures of the night sniff the air for the telltale odor of the badger before venturing out into the darkness, and it must be terrifying to hear a badger digging down from overhead. That is when those extra exits from a burrow come in most handy!

Mother watches while baby badger plays at the burrow entrance.

THE SPOTTED SKUNK

The small black-and-white spotted skunk leaves its rock-crevice den at dusk to hunt for mice or Jack rabbits in the moonlight. If the animals it prefers as food are scarce, the little skunk is satisfied to eat grasshoppers and crickets—or even cactus fruit. This small relative of the striped skunk, familiar to you in your back yard, is about half the size of a cat and weighs about one and a half pounds. It is far more active than its larger cousin but its appetite is less. Perhaps this is why the spotted skunk can make a living on waste ground, in gullies and rock slides, and in the desert itself. Even when hunting is poor, the animal seems to get along all right.

When frightened, this skunk can climb a tree, if there is one nearby, or run fast to his rock crevice, or even dodge into the entrance to a badger's den. But if cornered, it uses its "gas gun" with the same devastating effect as its larger relative. Sometimes it stands on its front feet alone, in order to aim higher, and any enemy that has been gassed gives the little skunk a wide berth forever after!

You may know this fellow as the "civet cat" and you may have watched it climb a mulberry or persimmon tree to gather fruit. It runs boldly about in the moonlight without any fear. If you should see one, keep your distance because its aim is good!

THE WILD PIG (PECCARY)

When the peccaries, those short-tempered, ferocious wild pigs, with their razor-sharp tusks, come crashing through the undergrowth toward the water hole, all the little animals disappear into the shadows. A band of pigs, consisting of any number from four to fifty, may be heard a hundred yards away, which, fortunately, serves as a warning to the nervous small creatures to leave the water hole hastily! No animal cares to meet a peccary band, not even a mountain lion.

The wild pigs crowd toward the water hole, making loud grunts and with much pushing, to get a drink. When their thirst is satisfied, they once more crash off into the shrubs, to eat whatever they can find, from cacti to snakes. Only after the the sound has died away do little heads appear once more from the shadows, and the rabbits and other shy creatures creep back to the water's edge. Then the doe and her fawns slip gracefully out from the darkness and all drink in peace.

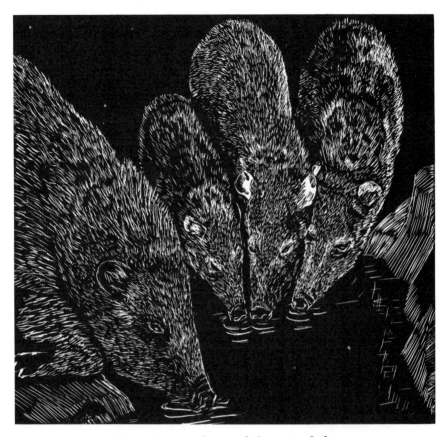

Peccaries crowd around the water hole.

THE MULE DEER

With dainty steps the mule deer advances toward the water hole. The large erect ears, which give this deer its name, twist constantly from side to side. The doe sniffs the air and, as if in answer to a signal that all is well, twin fawns step softly to her side. The three start to drink. The small animals nearby hear the deer and every one feels reassured. The Jack rabbit hops closer without fear.

The doe waits in the darkness, her large eyes wide and alert, until her fawns have finished drinking; then the trio disappear into the woods, just as quietly as they arrived. Throughout the night they browse on sagebrush, buffalo berry and other shrubs, with their long ears flapping. Suddenly, the doe raises her head, ears once more erect and turning about. At once the three deer bound away, clearing the brush and rock outcrops with long, graceful leaps. If a stalking coyote follows the doe too closely, she strikes out with her hoofs, for she is fearless when defending her fawns. But she must use her nose to tell if a cougar is near, for this creature is a silent hunter that walks on padded paws. The deer has no defense against its powerful spring but, when it comes to running, the mule deer is the champion.

If you should see the mule deer at a water hole, you will notice the beautiful set of branched antlers, and, although the animal is heavier than the white-tail deer, its grace of movement and long leaps cannot be surpassed.

THE COYOTE

Coyotes often gather on a small hill or rock ledge in the moonlight to "sing." Their chorus of howls and long-drawn-out wails breaks the silence of the desert and the plains night after night.

This member of the dog family prefers wide open spaces where it can stalk rabbits in the tall grass and chase antelopes across the meadows, or lie in wait behind a cactus bush for the kangaroo rat to jump past.

The coyote is larger than the fox but smaller than the wolf, and, like these relatives, it is a good "family" animal. A mated pair of coyotes stays together to train the young. Like the wolf and the fox, the male is a good provider and the female a

devoted mate. Together, they teach their pups by example how to hunt. Of course, the young animals are usually wild with excitement and jump about, yapping and getting in the way—just as the wolf and fox cubs do.

Yet the coyote is somewhat the poor relation among these wild dogs. Its fur is rough and coarse. It will tag behind other animals and take their leavings and will eat anything edible, from prickly pear (a cactus fruit) in the desert to grasshoppers in the fields and frogs in the ponds—and it has even been known to surprise a bear and grab its dinner.

Wherever the coyote lives, it serenades the stars each night. You may be familiar with its "song" and wonder what it means to the wild dog. Perhaps it just "sings" because it likes the sound of its own voice. It is as though the coyotes are saying, "Now let us all join in and sing," and "The more we are together, the merrier we will be!"

THE KIT FOX

The smallest, fastest and shiest of all foxes is the kit fox, which makes its underground den in the plains and deserts where the small, burrowing animals abound. There is sure to be a kit fox den near the mounds of the kangaroo rat, because the kit fox has a special liking for the little jumping creatures. The small fox will, of course, stalk a Jack rabbit if one is about. Whatever it manages to capture, it carries to its den to be eaten.

The den may be an abandoned home of a badger, or the fox may dig a new one of its own. Perhaps one of the reasons why this little fox can live so well in the desert is that the loose, sandy soil can be dug even by a fox that is by nature ill equipped for digging. In any case, the den becomes the permanent home and not just a nursery. The animal needs protection from the hot sun and desert winds during the daytime. The den is always supplied with several entrances so that it is always possible to escape from that champion of diggers, the badger himself.

Like other kinds of foxes, both parents are devoted to their young, and the male provides meat for the family until such time as the cubs are ready to join in the nightly hunting trips, when they learn how to catch pocket mice and kangaroo rats themselves.

If you should see a family of slender, buff-gray kit foxes at a water hole, you would notice how well the color of their fur blends with the desert background. The tips of the bushy tails are black, and their large ears are filled with hair, to keep out the desert dust when the winds whip up a storm. Because these little foxes are shy, they rarely visit the water hole to drink when other animals are around. The least noise sends them silently into the shadows.

THE COUGAR

The cougar, also called the panther, puma or mountain lion, is another big, wild relative of your cat. And like your cat, it hunts at dusk and through the night, with eyes that can make use of the faintest light—even starlight. It slinks along as it watches a herd of mule deer, just as your kitten creeps after a mouse or a moving leaf. When a deer strays a little apart from the others, the great cougar springs swiftly forward and strikes with its powerful paws. The deer falls and the rest of the herd scatters into the distance. After a hearty meal, the cougar carefully scrapes dry leaves over the remains and slips softly into the darkness. If there are young at home in the cave that serves as a den, a choice piece is carried along. If not, what is left will serve for a future meal.

If the great, buff-colored cat is unsuccessful in attempting a kill, it makes no attempt to pursue the fast-running deer but

turns to hunt for a fox or even a rabbit. The cougar moves slowly and carefully, its head swinging from side to side, its eyes alert for any movement on the ground or in the low trees and shrubs.

Everything about this wild cat reminds us of our household pets, although a male cougar may weigh as much as a grown man. The baby wild kittens roll and play like ordinary kittens. Their little claws are like needles—you know how sharp they can be, of course, for you have been scratched by a kitten, too.

The male animal leaves long, wide scratches on the bare earth as a message to the female. You may happen upon such a message in the daytime and, even though you can't read it, you will know you have missed seeing a big wild cat "write" it!

Cougars are found almost everywhere on the plains and in the mountains, in the woods, in the deserts and in the tropical forests. Wherever food is available, the great cat is to be found. It is bold and confident, for it has no enemies except man, but it is an enemy of all the other animals that live nearby.

Yes, the woods and desert, the fields and ponds, and even your own back yard and your city park, contain the homes and feeding grounds of animals that sleep while you are awake and live their active lives when you are tucked snugly in your bed. Now you know that during the daytime they are in their nests or burrows, waiting for darkness to fall and bring a feeling of protection before they come out in search of food.

No longer will you picture night as being empty, for you realize that birds and bats fly overhead in the dusk, moles and shrews dig busily underground, porcupines and opossums climb about in the treetops, mice scurry over the ground, looking for seeds, while owls listen and watch for any sound or movement before they swoop silently down.

Out there in the dark, baby skunks and raccoons follow their mothers around, learning their woodland lessons, and the doe quietly visits her fawns, hidden in a thicket.

You, too, can train your eyes to see movement in the shadows and your ears to catch the slightest sound. You can learn to distinguish the chirp of the cricket from the peeps of the frog, and the twittering of small birds from the squeals of the shrew. Most of all, you can learn to stand completely silent so that you will not frighten the night creatures. When you do this, a new world of wonder and adventure will be open to you.

Index

ABOUT THE AUTHOR

Jacquelyn Berrill was born in Kentucky, graduated from the University of Toledo, and did post graduate study at New York University. She was a group social worker with teen-age girls in the Jackson and Lansing, Michigan, Y.W.C.A., before her marriage to Dr. N. J. Berrill, professor of Zoology at McGill University, Montreal.

The Berrills have three children, Peggy, Elsilyn and Michael, ranging from college age to married. Now there is a new generation of young children to enjoy their grandmother's books. Besides keeping house and writing and illustrating her books Mrs. Berrill makes jewelry. This new hobby she finds completely fascinating.

The family spend their winters in the center of Montreal and their holidays at their home in Boothbay Harbor, Maine, where they have a cottage which they built themselves, and where the children have their own house on top of a large rock which the last glacier conveniently left in their back yard.